Qualifications and Credit Framework (QCF)

LEVEL 3 DIPLOMA IN ACCOUNTING

(QCF)

QUESTION BANK

Professional Ethics in Accounting and Finance

2010 Edition

First edition July 2010

ISBN 9780 7517 8824 2

British Library Cataloguing-in-Publication Data
A catalogue record for this book is available from the British Library

Published by

BPP Learning Media Ltd
BPP House
Aldine Place
London W12 8AA

www.bpp.com/learningmedia

Printed in the United Kingdom

CONTENTS

A NOTE ABOUT COPYRIGHT

INTRODUCTION

This is BPP Learning Media's AAT Question Bank for Professional Ethics in Accounting and Finance (PEAF). It is part of a suite of new ground breaking resources produced by BPP Learning Media for the AAT's new assessments under the qualification and credit framework.

The new PEAF assessment will be **computer assessed**. As well as being available in the traditional paper format, this **question bank is available in an online form** where all questions and assessments are presented in a **style which mimics the style of the AAT's assessments.** BPP Learning Media believe that the best way to practise for an online assessment is in an online environment. However, if you are unable to practise in the online environment you will find that all tasks in the paper question bank have been written in a style that is as close as possible to the style that you will be presented with in your online assessment.

This question bank has been written in conjunction with the BPP Text, and has been carefully designed to enable students to practise all of the learning outcomes and assessment criteria for the units that make up Professional Ethics in Accounting and Finance. It is fully up to date as at June 2010 and reflects both the AAT's unit guide and the sample assessment provided by the AAT.

This Question Bank contains these key features:

- questions corresponding to each chapter of the Text. Some are designed for learning purposes, others are of assessment standard

- the AAT's sample assessment and answers for Professional Ethics in Accounting and Finance, plus two further practice assessments

The emphasis in all tasks and assessments is on the practical application of the skills acquired.

If you have any comments about this book, please e-mail suedexter@bpp.com or write to Sue Dexter, Publishing Director, BPP Learning Media Ltd, BPP House, Aldine Place, London W12 8AA.

Question bank

Chapter 1

Task 1.1

You have recently been helping a corporate client prepare for a takeover of another company. The bid has been a success and the directors of your client are delighted to have acquired this other company at what they consider to be a very good price. In order to thank you for your help in this matter, you and your husband have been offered an all expenses paid week in the company villa in Portugal.

Should you accept this offer or not?

- Yes
- No

Task 1.2

A client of your company has just moved their business to another firm. Some time ago, they requested your manager to send over the client's books and records. He did not. Each time they called to chase up the request, it seems that the manager 'screened' their call and never responded.

What fundamental ethical principle does this situation raise?

- Integrity
- Professional competence and due care
- Professional behaviour

Task 1.3

You work for a firm of chartered accountants and are required to fill out a time sheet to record each hour worked for each client each day. Last Friday you forgot to prepare the sheet for the week, and you are now doing it on Monday morning. However you are not absolutely sure how long you worked for each client on Thursday and Friday as due to pressure of work you did not record it.

What fundamental ethical principle does this situation raise?

- Integrity
- Confidentiality
- Professional behaviour

Task 1.4

While at a party at the weekend, you meet a client of yours who is clearly very concerned about some VAT issues. You know enough about VAT to carry out your daily work, but you are not an expert on the areas of imports and exports on which your client is asking your opinion.

What ethical issue does this situation raise?

- Objectivity
- Professional competence and due care
- Professional behaviour

Task 1.5

Which of the following is the best definition of the AAT's Guidelines on Professional Ethics 'conceptual framework'?

- A set of definitions of the fundamental ethical principles

- A problem solving procedure that can be used to give you the best chance of complying with ethical principles

- A set of rules to follow when deciding whether or not to consult the AAT Director of Professional Development

Task 1.6

'As a professional, you should behave with courtesy and consideration towards anyone with whom you come into contact.'

Which of the fundamental ethical principles does this illustrate?

- Integrity
- Professional competence and due care
- Professional behaviour

Task 1.7

You have strong views in support of a client who is being threatened with legal action by a supplier who is alleging late payment of invoices. You have offered to state publicly your views on the matter, in defence of your client.

What type of threat to independence does this situation represent?

- Self-interest threat
- Familiarity threat
- Advocacy threat

Task 1.8

Categorise the following safeguards according to whether they are created by the profession, or are present in the work environment:

Profession	Work environment

- Rotation of personnel
- Appointment of an ethics officer
- Continuing professional development
- Corporate governance regulations
- Quality controls
- Internal audits
- Professional standards
- Third-party review of financial reports
- Mechanisms to protect whistle-blowers

Task 1.9

A 'rules based' approach to ethical problem solving has the advantage that because things are clear-cut, leaving no room for misunderstanding, it is easier to know what to do. Which of the following are DISADVANTAGES of such an approach?

- Conflicting interests and priorities must be carefully balanced

- It sets more rigorous standards of behaviour, and so needs a lot of resources

- There is a higher risk of getting swamped by the details and missing the bigger picture

Task 1.10

In the UK, which part of the Financial Reporting Council acts as a tribunal and can impose fines and other sanctions against accountants whose work fails to measure up to professional standards?

- The Accounting Standards Board (ASB)
- The Accountancy and Actuarial Discipline Board (AADB)
- The Professional Oversight Board (POB)

Task 1.11

Complete the following statement by dragging the appropriate word(s) to each gap in the sentence:

'IFAC is an --------- body representing all the major ---------- bodies across the world. Its mission is to develop the high --------- of professional accountants and enhance the ------- of services they provide.'

professional	international	cost	standards	accountancy	quality

Task 1.12

Which of the following members of the CCAB is a sponsoring member of the AAT?

- ICAI
- ACCA
- CIMA

Task 1.13

Identify whether the following business values are those set out in the Nolan Principles, by dragging a relevant item to the boxes:

Nolan Principles

Business values

Trust
Accountability
Transparency
Accuracy
Selflessness
Honesty

Task 1.14

Monty, a member in practice, performs bookkeeping services for both Stumpy Ltd and Grind Ltd. The companies are in dispute about a series of sales that Stumpy Ltd made to Grind Ltd.

Complete the following sentence by selecting the appropriate option:

'For Monty, this situation threatens the fundamental principles of

- Integrity and due care'
- Confidentiality and professional behaviour'
- Objectivity and confidentiality'

Task 1.15

What is the name of the body that regulates the financial services industry in the UK?

- The Financial Services Association
- The Financial Services Authority
- The Accounting Standards Board

Task 1.16

Complete the following statement by dragging the appropriate word(s) to each gap in the sentence:

'A(n) -------- is a person who acts as an -------- between an organisation and the general public.

'A(n) -------- is an informal name given to --------- protection organisations or campaigners.

intermediary	ombudsman	consumer	agent	watchdog	government

Task 1.17

Match the terms by dragging into the appropriate box:

Code of conduct	Code of practice

- Designed to influence the behaviour of employees
- Adopted by a profession or organisation to regulate that profession

Task 1.18

Complete the following statement by dragging the appropriate word(s) to each gap in the sentence:

The Basel Committee on Banking Supervision (BCBS) defines -------- risk as: 'The risk of -------- resulting from inadequate or failed internal --------, people and systems or from -------- events.'

international	operational	loss	standards	processes	external

Task 1.19

John has been found guilty of professional misconduct by an AAT Disciplinary Tribunal. Which of the following is a possible penalty that he could face?

- Expelled from the Association
- A conviction under the criminal law and imprisonment
- Fined an unlimited sum

Task 1.20

Put the AAT's Four-stage cycle for CPD into order, by dragging the relevant stages to the relevant boxes:

The AAT's Four-step cycle for CPD

Step 1:
Step 2:
Step 3:
Step 4:

The learning stages

Evaluate the outcomes at the year end
Plan the learning activity you will undertake
Assess your learning and development needs for the year
Put the learning plan into action

Chapter 2

Task 2.1

James, an AAT member in practice, has decided to open his own practice, and as a first marketing step he has decided that his fees will be on average 20% lower than those of his competitors. What issue does this promotional tool give rise to?

- None – he can charge what he likes
- It is unethical to charge a lot lower than competitors
- James should make sure that he can provide a quality service for that price

Task 2.2

Ruchita, an AAT member, has asked you to comment on her ideas for marketing her services. She wants to call her business 'Ruchita MAAT International – Biggest is Best', as she says that she has several tax clients who have moved overseas but are retaining her services for their UK affairs. You tell her that you think the name may be misleading – in what particular ways?

- She cannot use her own name

- The word 'International' implies a certain size

- She cannot use 'MAAT' under section 253.5 of the AAT Guidelines on Professional Ethics

- She must put 'Taxation Services' in the business name

- 'Biggest is Best' is subjective and difficult to prove

Task 2.3

Ruchita also wants to offer financial incentives to third parties to introduce clients to her business. What principles must she adhere to?

- This should not be done at all, as such arrangements are unethical
- The clients must be made aware of the payments
- The third party needs to be trusted to carry out the introduction with integrity
- Ruchita does not have to pay the third party if the client is not a good one

Task 2.4

Select the most appropriate response from the list:

'In the UK context of the receiving and paying of commissions when introducing clients, the relationship between a client and adviser is regarded as a ...

- Professional relationship; you must maintain professional standards'

- Confidential relationship; you cannot divulge any information about commissions paid or received'

- Fiduciary relationship; you must hand commissions received over to the client'

Task 2.5

Complete the following statement by dragging the appropriate word(s) to each gap in the sentence:

The ------- Regulations 2007 require you to exercise 'due diligence' in gathering information about a prospective customer, including:

- The client's -------, verified by appropriate identification and/or references

- ------- information, including its expected patterns of business, its business model and its source of funds.

Know your client	Money Laundering	confidential	Anti-Corruption	acceptable	identity

Task 2.6

What does the acronym SOCA stand for?

- Serious Organised Crime Association
- Scene of Crime Authority
- Serious Organised Crime Agency
- Scene of Crime Association

Task 2.7

What are the key purposes of a letter of engagement?

- Provides written confirmation of the agreement with the client
- Provides details of all current and future work engagements
- Outlines the responsibilities of both the client and the accountant in the relationship
- Manages client expectations

Task 2.8

- In which circumstance should an AAT member ensure a new letter of engagement is needed for an existing client?

- When the practice is to provide consultancy services to the client when it currently only provides them with audit services

- At the start of every tax year where the practice provides the client with tax advice

- Annually, regardless of whether any new services are provided or the terms of existing services are changed

Task 2.9

A client has told you informally that she expects to inherit from a recently deceased relative. You initially declined to advise her informally on tax matters since you were not sure of your expertise. However, she has now received a considerable sum from the relative's estate, and wants to consult you on the best thing for her to do with the money.

What is your position here?

- This amounts to a request for investment advice, and you are not qualified to give it
- You can give her general advice on what most people do with large inheritances
- You can point her in the direction of your cousin, who is a financial advisor

Task 2.10

A client is trying to sell her floristry business, and has asked you to prepare financial statements for the business (income and expenditure account, balance sheet and a 5-year cash flow forecast) for a potential buyer that she has found. She has asked that you base your fee upon the eventual selling price of the business.

What is your position here?

- Contingent fees are never permitted under the AAT's Ethical Guidelines

- You can offer financial reporting services on a contingent fee basis, as long as you disclose the fee to the appropriate authority

- You cannot offer financial reporting services on a contingent fee basis as this represents a threat to your objectivity

Task 2.11

Where an AAT member enters into an agency relationship with a client this may present a threat to their professional ▬▬▬.

- Independence
- Standards
- Behaviour

Task 2.12

A client contacts you after you have both signed a letter of engagement, and says that in addition to the services detailed in this letter he would like you to calculate his tax liabilities with regard to the upcoming sale of his property investments. You propose that you draw up a new letter of engagement to cover this additional task. 'But it will still be included in the fee we agreed, won't it?' the client asks.

What is the correct response to your client?

- The original fee was based on the estimated time it would take to complete a different set of tasks, so a new fee must be negotiated
- There is no need to negotiate a new fee as the work will be covered by the original letter of engagement
- You should propose a fee based upon the outcome of the tax liability calculations

Task 2.13

A member of the public has asked you as an AAT member to provide them with a second opinion on advice they have received from another firm. However you will not have access to the books and records the other firm used to prepare their advice because they are still holding onto them.

If you were to provide a second opinion without these books and records then this would be in breach of which fundamental principle?

- Confidentiality
- Professional competence and due care
- Objectivity

Task 2.14

'Pre-arranged fees are not a good idea, as it is impossible to tell what may happen during an assignment.'

- True
- False

Task 2.15

Keith, a member in practice, wishes to enter into a professional relationship with a client.

Answer the following question by selecting the appropriate option:

As part of his customer due diligence processes, which of the following actions must Keith take?

- Verify the validity of the client's business model and cashflow data
- Verify the client's identity
- Notify the FRC of the proposed relationship

Task 2.16

Johnny, an AAT member in practice, has been accused of bringing the profession into disrepute through the marketing of his practice.

Complete the following sentence by selecting the appropriate option:

'This accusation is most likely to be upheld if Johnny

- states in an advertisement that he is a fully qualified member of the AAT'

- includes his photograph on his letterhead'

- makes an uncomplimentary reference in his advertising to the work of a member of the ICAS'

Task 2.17

An AAT member can be said to be acting fairly in which of the following circumstances?

- They avoid using their work phone for making personal calls
- They avoid discriminating against others
- They respect another's right of confidentiality.

Task 2.18

Which of the following represents a self-interest threat for an AAT member in business?

- Having an opportunity to use company assets for own advantage

- Being asked to justify a decision where they were involved in preparing information on which the decision is based

- Having a long association with a business contact

Task 2.19

Which of the following represents an advocacy threat to an AAT member in practice?

- Promoting shares in a listed company which they audit
- Depending on a client's fees for a significant portion of their income
- Discovering a significant error when re-evaluating their work

Task 2.20

Bob, a senior AAT member working as a partner in a large practice, has a client who runs a newsagent – but he has heard that another of his clients, a bookshop, is planning to open its own outlet in direct competition. There is clearly going to be a conflict of interest between the two clients.

What should Bob do?

- Inform both clients of the potential for conflict, promise them confidentiality and leave it at that

- No action is required – as a senior member of the practice, Bob is fully aware of the potential for conflicts of interest and will act accordingly

- Propose a 'Chinese wall' by handing the bookshop client to another team at another office; inform both clients of the changes

Chapter 3

Task 3.1

Why is professional independence particularly important in assurance services?

- Independence is necessary to enable the member to express a conclusion that is free of bias
- Independence is necessary to enable the member to charge a realistic fee
- Independence is necessary to enable the member to gain access to confidential and sensitive information

Task 3.2

A long association with a business contact, which may influence your decisions, is best described as which type of threat to objectivity and independence?

- Self-interest
- Intimidation
- Familiarity

Task 3.3

Which of the following represents a potential threat to your objectivity?

- Unfamiliar software or systems
- Your uncle is the Finance Director at your main competitor
- Inaccurate information from colleagues when preparing an important report

Task 3.4

Complete the following statement by dragging the appropriate word(s) to the gap in the sentence:

'________ are attempts to influence somebody's decisions or actions.'

- Gifts
- Inducements
- Offers of hospitality

Task 3.5

What is 'independence of mind'?

- The willingness to avoid situations that could pose questions as to your ability to be objective

- The ability to put aside all considerations that are not relevant to the decision or task at hand

Task 3.6

Choose the most accurate response from the list below:

Serena has been offered a bottle of wine for her wine connoisseur husband as a Christmas gift by a client, in appreciation of her work. Is she correct to accept the gift?

- Yes – the gift is for her husband, not her

- No – it is never correct to accept gifts from clients

- Yes – the gift is not likely to be perceived as significant enough to affect her objectivity

Task 3.7

Choose the most appropriate responses to complete the sentence below.

The husband of Jessica, a member in practice, has made a large loan to Laing Ltd, where Jessica is currently working on an assurance engagement.

'This situation presents a

- Familiarity threat
- Self-interest threat

and the best course of action would be

- To remove Jessica from the assurance engagement'
- To inform the audit committee of Laing Ltd'

Task 3.8

Fill in the blank:

If you are employed by a public body in the UK, the acceptance of gifts may be illegal under -----------

- Accountancy profession ethical codes
- Anti-corruption legislation
- The Nolan principles

Task 3.9

Under the Fraud Act 2006 a person found guilty of fraud can be punished by a prison sentence or a fine.

- True
- False

Task 3.10

Sarah, an AAT member working in a manufacturing company, has been asked to prepare detailed financial information on a new product of which she has very little knowledge. The accountant who normally deals with this product is away on leave for several weeks, and the information is required urgently as part of a report to shareholders. Sarah is very unsure about her ability to complete the work to her usual high standards.

What should she do in this situation?

- Take on the challenge, and use the opportunity to impress her colleagues

- Let her manager know that the task is outside the boundaries of her expertise and experience

- Ask for all the information that is available on the new product and ask her friend in another company to do it for her

Task 3.11

Robert, an AAT member, holds a number of shares in his employing company, and has become eligible for a profit-related bonus for the first time. What type of threat could this represent to his objectivity when preparing company financial statements?

- Self-interest
- Self-review
- Intimidation

Task 3.12

Complete the following statement by dragging the appropriate word(s) to the gaps in the sentence:

When preparing financial statements, there is a clear need to apply the principles of ------- (not disclosing sensitive information), ---------- (preparing and presenting information in accordance with financial reporting and other applicable professional standards) and ------ (presenting information free of bias or self interest).

- Objectivity
- Competence and due care
- Confidentiality

Task 3.13

A new client has asked you to hold a significant amount of money but has declined to tell you what the purpose of this money is.

Would you accept this money?

- Yes; it must be held in a separate bank account

- No; you do not know the purpose of the funds

- No; you cannot accept monies from new clients until they have been with you for more than two years

Task 3.14

Glen, an AAT member, has just started his own tax advisory business. One of his clients, Joanne, has asked him to keep custody of £25,000 in cash for one month, when it will need to be paid to HM Revenue and Customs.

What should Glen do?

- Hold the money separately from that of his business
- Inform Joanne that he cannot hold the money
- Keep a note of the amount of money, but hold it in his established bank account

Task 3.15

Gregory is an AAT member in practice who acts as account signatory on behalf of a client, Natalie, who is frequently out of the country and non-contactable on long business trips. Last month Greg transferred £7,000 to himself from one of Natalie's many bank accounts.

Answer the following question by selecting the appropriate option:

Which Fraud Act 2006 offence is it most likely that Gregory has committed?

- Fraud by false representation
- Fraud by failing to disclose information
- Fraud by abuse of position

Task 3.16

Saskia is an AAT member in practice, employed by Evans LLP. She has recently completed an assurance engagement at Lawrence Ltd. Lawrence Ltd is no longer a client of Evans LLP, but Saskia has acquired some information about it that would be of interest to another client, DH Ltd.

Complete the following sentence by selecting the appropriate option from the dropdown menu:

'The principle of confidentiality

- Imposes an obligation on Saskia not to disclose the information to DH Ltd'
- Imposes no obligation on Saskia: Lawrence Ltd is no longer a client'
- Imposes an obligation on Saskia, but her assistant is free to disclose'

Task 3.17

Paul is an AAT member who acts as a principal in relation to his client, Sue Ltd. Paul has agreed to prepare the purchase ledger control account reconciliation as a one-off service to assist with the year end procedures.

Complete the following sentence by selecting the appropriate option:

'Ownership of the reconciliation when it is complete is

- Paul's'
- Sue Ltd's'

Task 3.18

Peter is an AAT member who acts as a principal in relation to his client, Mary Ltd. Peter has been involved in lengthy correspondence with Jones Ltd, regarding consultancy work that Jones Ltd undertook for Mary Ltd, and which Peter is investigating.

Complete the following sentence by selecting the appropriate option:

'Ownership of this correspondence with Jones Ltd belongs to

- Peter'
- Mary Ltd'

Task 3.19

Identify the three conditions that must exist for John, an AAT member, to have a right of lien over the documents of his client, Elton Ltd:

A right of lien exists

Conditions

The documents belong to Elton Ltd
The documents are Elton Ltd's statutory books and accounting records
The documents are in John's possession because he has been working on them
The documents are being held by John after being left at his office by Elton Ltd by mistake
Work has been done by John on the documents and the fee has been paid
Work has been done by John on the documents, but the fee is outstanding

Task 3.20

Complete the following sentence by selecting the appropriate option:

Failure by a member in practice of the duty to exercise reasonable care and skill means the member may be liable for

- fraud, leading to a claim for compensation
- professional negligence, leading to a claim for damages
- breach of duty of care, and a claim for compensation

Chapter 4

Task 4.1

If you are employed by an organisation, where should you take any ethical concerns in the first instance if you cannot resolve them with the other person concerned?

- Your immediate supervisor as part of an ethical reporting procedure
- The AAT Ethics Advice Line
- Independent legal expert

Task 4.2

Fill in the blank:

When you submit a tax return or computations for a client or employer, you are acting as ──────── of the taxpayer.

- Principal
- Agent

Task 4.3

Fred, an AAT member, is preparing tax computations for his client, Barney Ltd. It is ──────── who bears ultimate responsibility for the accuracy of the data and computations.

- Barney Ltd
- Fred

Task 4.4

Pat, an AAT member in practice, has become aware of a significant error in a tax return from a previous year for one of her clients, Connor Ltd. What should she do?

- Immediately advise Connor Ltd – and recommend that they inform HMRC
- Make the disclosure herself
- Resign from the appointment

Task 4.5

Under-declaring income and over-declaring expenses on a tax computation can lead to accusations of money laundering.

- True
- False

Task 4.6

Sam, an AAT member, has misgivings over one of his clients, Avalon Ltd. He believes that there is undeclared income and has asked the owners to supply him with a general assurance, in writing, that all income is being declared. It is now time to prepare Avalon Ltd's tax return. How should Sam approach his next meeting with the client?

- Assure them that he is 'on their side' and will get them the best tax refund that he possibly can

- Ensure that they understand that they bear ultimate responsibility for the accuracy of the facts, information and tax computations, and that he can refuse to be associated with their tax return if he suspects that it is incomplete or inaccurate

- Tell them that he cannot act for them any more as he believes that they are not declaring their full income

Task 4.7

When an AAT member faces a conflict between professional standards and his or her duty towards an employer (for example if the employer asks that a misleading tax return be submitted), what should take priority?

- The rules and standards of the profession take priority
- The employer's objectives should be put first

Task 4.8

While an AAT member may seek independent or professional advice on an ethical matter, he or she is still bound by a duty of ‐‐‐‐‐‐‐

- Confidentiality
- Competence
- Co-operation

Task 4.9

For a member in practice, if a client requests or instructs you to take a course of action that is unethical or illegal, what should you do?

- Refuse to take that course of action
- Immediately cease to act for that client

Task 4.10

Jimmy, an AAT member, has been employed for some years by Laura LLP. He feels that his department manager Nadia poses a threat to his ability to perform his duties with the appropriate degree of professional behaviour, as she keeps asking him to falsify his timesheets so that she can charge higher fees to clients. Jimmy wishes to make a disclosure to senior management at Laura LLP.

Answer the following question by selecting the appropriate option:

What is Jimmy's position as a whistle-blower in relation to the Public Interest Disclosure Act?

- He will be protected provided he acts in good faith
- He will not be protected unless he discloses to a legal adviser
- He will not be protected as this is a breach of confidentiality

Task 4.11

Answer the following question by selecting the appropriate option:

Which of the following disclosures does the Public Interest Disclosure Act 1998 cover?

- Professional negligence
- Endangerment of an individual's health and safety
- Breach of contract

Task 4.12

Savya is an AAT member on an assurance engagement at Paint plc. During the course of the engagement he has heard client staff talking about certain funds, which Savya now believes derive from tax evasion.

Complete the following sentence by selecting the appropriate option:

'Savya must report his suspicions so as to avoid a charge of

- Professional negligence'
- Failure to report'
- Breach of confidentiality'

Task 4.13

Why should written records be kept of discussions and meetings on ethical issues?

- To avoid allegations of professional misconduct
- To ensure that there is evidence of any advice received
- To send to the AAT Director of Professional Development

Task 4.14

Wilma, an AAT member, is leaving her employment with Betty Ltd after a disagreement with her manager over his handling of a bad working relationship with a colleague in the sales department. She has made the reasons for her resignation clear to her employer in her exit interview, and she wants to go to the local newspaper about what she sees as Betty Ltd's failure to listen to her concerns.

What is Wilma's position?

- Wilma is bound by a duty of confidentiality not to talk about her reasons for leaving
- Wilma is entitled to talk to the local paper about her treatment by Betty Ltd
- Wilma can sue Betty Ltd for breach of contract

Task 4.15

What two factors need to be balanced when considering whether or not to 'blow the whistle'?

- Confidentiality and objectivity
- Competence and public interest
- Confidentiality and public interest
- Duty of care and confidentiality

Task 4.16

Susie, an AAT member employed by Luna plc, is facing significant pressure from her manager to give incorrect information to the company's internal auditors.

Complete the following sentence by selecting the appropriate option from each dropdown menu:

'Susie's situation represents

- an intimidation threat
- an advocacy threat

and her immediate response should be to implement the safeguard of

- obtaining advice from the AAT'
- refusing to co-operate with the internal audit'

Task 4.17

You are aware that the retail company that you work for has taken on a full time sales person for its new shop, but when checking the payroll records you can find no mention of this new employee, nor any payments to her.

What is the first thing that you should do in this situation?

- Nothing – the arrangements between the shop and the employee are not your responsibility

- Speak to the payroll department, warning them about the risks of payroll fraud

- Speak to your manager

Task 4.18

Arousha, an AAT member, has been asked by her boss to include information in an important report to the Board of Directors that she knows to be inaccurate. What type of threat does this represent, and what should she do as a first step?

- Intimidation threat; seek legal advice
- Self-review threat; resign
- Intimidation threat; refuse to be associated with the information
- Self-review threat; seek legal advice

Task 4.19

Which of the following constitutes money laundering?

- Benefits obtained through bribery
- Delaying payments to suppliers for as long as possible
- Using of client money to pay outstanding fees

Task 4.20

What is 'tipping off'?

- Disclosing something that might prejudice an investigation
- Advising clients on the prevention of money laundering
- Disclosing suspicion of money laundering activity to the appropriate authorities

Answer bank

Answer bank

Chapter 1

Task 1.1

NO. This offer of a free holiday should not be accepted due to the principles of professional behaviour and objectivity. The offer is of significant value. Such a gift, if accepted, could be seen from an observer's point of view as payment in kind for special favours, or may indicate that you may be biased towards that client in future.

Task 1.2

This is simply unprofessional behaviour by your manager. You may consider reporting the matter to your in-house ethics committee, if there is one.

Task 1.3

From a personal point of view this is a matter of integrity. Your clients are charged fees on the basis of the hours that you and other members of the firm work for them, so it is important that the recording of these hours is accurate. Therefore you are right to be concerned about not knowing the precise hours, and should ensure that this situation does not happen again.

Task 1.4

This raises issues of professional competence and due care. You know that you do not have the knowledge to answer these questions at this time and in this situation. For your own professional safety, you should make the client clearly aware of this and not be prepared to give any opinion, as this may be relied upon by the client despite the circumstances. The most appropriate form of action would be to make an appointment with the client to discuss the matter properly after you have done some research into these specific areas, or refer them to a colleague with experience in this area.

Task 1.5

A problem solving procedure that can be used to give you the best chance of complying with ethical principles

Task 1.6

Professional behaviour. 'The principle of professional behaviour imposes an obligation on members to comply with relevant laws and regulations and avoid any action that may bring disrepute to the profession.'

Task 1.7

Advocacy threat. The risk is that, since you are prepared to promote your opinion, people will have difficulty in believing that you are objective.

Task 1.8

Profession	Work environment
Continuing professional development	Quality controls
Corporate governance regulations	Internal audits
Professional standards	Mechanisms to protect whistle-blowers
Third-party review of financial reports	Rotation of personnel
	Appointment of an ethics officer

Task 1.9

There is a higher risk of getting swamped by the details and missing the bigger picture

Tasks 1.10

The Accountancy and Actuarial Discipline Board (AADB)

Tasks 1.11

'IFAC is an **international** body representing all the major **accountancy** bodies across the world. Its mission is to develop the high **standards** of professional accountants and enhance the **quality** of services they provide.'

Task 1.12

CIMA

Task 1.13

Accountability
Selflessness
Honesty

Task 1.14

Objectivity and confidentiality'

Task 1.15

The Financial Services Authority

Task 1.16

'An **ombudsman** is a person who acts as an **intermediary** between an organisation and the general public.

'A **watchdog** is an informal name given to **consumer** protection organisations or campaigners.

Task 1.17

Code of conduct	Code of practice
Designed to influence the behaviour of employees	Adopted by a profession or organisation to regulate that profession

Task 1.18

The Basel Committee on Banking Supervision (BCBS) defines **operational** risk as: 'The risk of **loss** resulting from inadequate or failed internal **processes**, people and systems or from **external** events.'

Task 1.19

John may be expelled from the Association. There cannot be a criminal conviction as failing to follow the AAT's Guidelines is not a criminal offence. He may be fined, but there is a maximum amount which is set by the council so it cannot be unlimited

Task 1.20

Step 1: Assess your learning and development needs for the year

Step 2: Plan the learning activity you will undertake

Step 3: Put the learning plan into action

Step 4: Evaluate the outcomes at the year end

Chapter 2

Task 2.1

James should make sure that he can provide a quality service for that price. If fees are mentioned in promotional material, James must ensure that the statements are not misleading, e.g. about what is covered and how the fees are calculated.

Task 2.2

- The word 'International' implies a certain size
- She cannot use 'MAAT' under section 253.5 of the Ethical Guidelines
- 'Biggest is Best' is subjective and difficult to prove

Task 2.3

- The clients must be made aware of the payments
- The third party needs to be trusted to carry out the introduction with integrity

Task 2.4

Fiduciary relationship; you must hand commissions received over to the client. In the UK, if you receive a commission for introducing a client to another firm, and you are the client's professional adviser (regarded in UK law as a 'fiduciary relationship'), you are legally bound to hand the money over to the client – unless they specifically approve your keeping it.

Task 2.5

The **Money Laundering** Regulations 2007 require you to exercise 'due diligence' in gathering information about a prospective customer, including:

- The client's **identity**, verified by appropriate identification and/or references.

- **'Know your client'** information, including its expected patterns of business, its business model and its source of funds.

Task 2.6

Serious Organised Crime Agency

Task 2.7

- Provides written confirmation of the agreement with the client
- Outlines the responsibilities of both the client and the accountant in the relationship
- Manages client expectations

Task 2.8

When the practice is to provide consultancy services to the client when it currently only provides them with audit services.

A new engagement letter is only required when a new assignment is undertaken, additional tasks are added to an existing assignment or the terms of the engagement are altered.

Task 2.9

This amounts to a request for investment advice, and you are not qualified to give it.

Task 2.10

You cannot offer financial reporting services on a contingent fee basis as this represents a threat to your objectivity.

Fees that depend on the outcome of an assignment are known as contingency fees and they must not be charged for financial reporting services as in this example.

Task 2.11

Independence. Before accepting an agency, members should be satisfied that their professional independence will not be compromised, and that acceptance is appropriate.

Task 2.12

The original fee was based on the estimated time it would take to complete a different set of tasks, so a new fee must be negotiated.

Fees must be based on the services that are to be provided. Where new services are added then specific fees which relate to them must be negotiated.

Task 2.13

Professional competence and due care.

Professional competence is at risk if you do not base your opinion on the same set of facts as the other accountant or if you have insufficient evidence to make a decision.

Task 2.14

False. Pre-arranged fees are quite acceptable, as long as the fee is fair for the work – and the work is fulfilled on that basis.

Task 2.15

Verify the client's identity.

Accountants should verify the identity of any new clients.

Task 2.16

Makes an uncomplimentary reference in his advertising to the work of a member of the ICAS. Members must never make disparaging references to, or comparisons with, the practice or services of others.

Task 2.17

They avoid discriminating against others

Not using a work phone for personal calls is an example of being honest. Respecting another's right to confidentiality is an example of sensitivity.

Task 2.18

Having an opportunity to use company assets for own advantage

Being asked to justify a decision where they were involved in preparing information on which the decision is based is an example of a self-review threat.

Having a long association with a business contact can create a familiarity threat.

Task 2.19

Promoting shares in a listed company which they audit.

- Depending on a client's fees for a significant portion of their income is an example of a self-interest threat.

- Discovering a significant error when re-evaluating their work is an example of a self-review threat.

Task 2.20

Propose a 'Chinese wall' by handing the bookshop client to another team at another office; inform both clients of the changes. It may also be prudent to insert a paragraph into new engagement letters, stating that 'all information will be kept confidential, except as required by law, regulatory or ethical guidance, and the client permits the firm to take such steps as the firm thinks fit to preserve confidentiality.'

Chapter 3

Task 3.1

Independence is necessary to enable the member to express a conclusion that is free of bias.

Task 3.2

Familiarity

Task 3.3

Your uncle being the competitor's Finance Director is more likely to be a threat to your *objectivity*. All of the other options represent potential threats to professional competence.

Task 3.4

Inducements. They may be made to encourage dishonest behaviour or to gain confidential information.

Task 3.5

The ability to put aside all considerations that are not relevant to the decision or task at hand. This is, essentially, objectivity – free from bias, prejudice or partiality.

Task 3.6

Yes – the gift is not likely to be perceived as significant enough to affect her objectivity.

Task 3.7

'This situation presents a self-interest threat and the best course of action would be to remove Jessica from the assurance engagement'.

Task 3.8

If you are employed by a public body in the UK, the acceptance of gifts may be illegal under **anti-corruption legislation**.

Task 3.9

True – fraud is a criminal offence punishable by imprisonment or a fine.

Task 3.10

Let her manager know that the task is outside the boundaries of her expertise and experience. It is important to be realistic and responsible and let people know when you are not confident about completing a task, especially when it is a significant one.

Task 3.11

Self-interest. If such threats are significant (i.e. the interest is direct and of high value), safeguards will have to be put in place.

Task 3.12

When preparing financial statements, there is a clear need to apply the principles of **confidentiality** (not disclosing sensitive information), **competence and due care** (preparing and presenting information in accordance with financial reporting and other applicable professional standards) and **objectivity** (presenting information free of bias or self-interest).

Task 3.13

No; you do not know the purpose of the funds. In this case you cannot accept the monies, as you cannot hold clients' monies without verifying the commercial purpose of the transaction.

Task 3.14

Hold the money separately from that of his business. Clients' monies should be kept separately from monies belonging to the member personally and/or to the practice.

Task 3.15

Fraud by abuse of position

Task 3.16

The principle of confidentiality imposes an obligation on Saskia not to disclose the information to DH Ltd. It applies even after the assignment, or the contractual relationship with the client is over. It applies not just to members, but also to any staff under their supervision.

Task 3.17

Sue Ltd's. Documents that have been created by a principal on the specific instructions of the client belong to the client.

Task 3.18

Peter. Letters exchanged with third parties belong to the principal.

Task 3.19

- The documents belong to Elton Ltd
- The documents are in John's possession because he has been working on them
- Work has been done by John on the documents, but the fee is outstanding

Task 3.20

Professional negligence, leading to a claim for damages

Chapter 4

Task 4.1

Your immediate supervisor as part of an ethical reporting procedure.

Task 4.2

Agent

Task 4.3

Barney Ltd

Task 4.4

Immediately advise Connor Ltd – and recommend that they inform HMRC.

Task 4.5

True – for the purposes of money laundering provisions, the proceeds of deliberate tax evasion are just as much 'criminal property' as money from drug trafficking or theft.

Task 4.6

Ensure that they understand that they are responsible for making full and accurate disclosure to the tax authorities.

Task 4.7

The rules and standards of the profession take priority

Task 4.8

Confidentiality

Task 4.9

Refuse to take that course of action (and perhaps explain the ethical or professional principles involved, in an attempt to get the client to change their mind)

Task 4.10

He will be protected provided he acts in good faith

Task 4.11

Endangerment of an individual's health and safety

Task 4.12

Failure to report

Task 4.13

To ensure that there is evidence of any advice received. This will help to protect you in any legal proceedings that may result; if your subsequent conduct is prosecuted, for example – or if you are unfairly victimised or dismissed for taking a stand on the issue.

Task 4.14

Wilma is bound by a duty of confidentiality not to talk about her reasons for leaving, as there does not appear to be any legal duty to disclose what has happened.

Task 4.15

Confidentiality and public interest. Whistle-blowing is the disclosure by an employee of illegal or unethical practices by his or her employer. This can be in the public interest – but confidentiality is also a very strong value to consider.

Task 4.16

Susie's situation represents an intimidation threat and her immediate response should be to implement the safeguard of obtaining advice from the AAT

Task 4.17

Your first step is probably to speak to your manager about your concerns, and it may then be suggested that you speak to the payroll department in general terms about the importance of accurate reporting. In this situation you will probably be suspicious that the employee is being paid in cash in order to avoid the tax consequences of employment. Payroll fraud is an offence that is reportable to SOCA.

Task 4.18

This is an intimidation threat, and as a first step she should refuse to be associated with incorrect information. If her manager persists in his request, Arousha may need to take legal advice.

Task 4.19

Benefits obtained through bribery. Money laundering is a process by which criminals attempt to conceal the true origin and ownership of the proceeds of their criminal activity.

Task 4.20

Disclosing something that might prejudice an investigation

SAMPLE ASSESSMENT
PROFESSIONAL ETHICS IN
ACCOUNTING AND FINANCE

Time allowed: 1 hour 30 minutes

PEAF Sample Assessment

Section 1

Task 1.1

Complete the following sentences by selecting the appropriate option from each dropdown menu.

(a) 'The behaviour of a member who is straightforward and honest in all professional and business relationships is following the fundamental principle of

- Objectivity'
- Professional competence and due care'
- Integrity'

(b) 'The conceptual framework approach requires members to

- Comply with a set of specific rules'

- Identify, evaluate and respond to threats to compliance with the fundamental principles'

Task 1.2

Answer the following questions by selecting the appropriate option in each case.

(a) The accountancy profession is committed to which of the following objectives?

- An outlook which is essentially commercial, achieved by being business minded and free from regulatory pressure

- Rendering services to acceptable standards of conduct and performance

- Acknowledgement of duties to society as a whole in addition to duties to the employer or client

(b) In the UK, which part of the Financial Reporting Council has direct responsibility for reviewing the way in which the professional accountancy bodies regulate their members?

- The Accounting Standards Board (ASB)
- The Accountancy and Actuarial Discipline Board (AADB)
- The Professional Oversight Board (POB)

Complete the following sentence by selecting the appropriate option from the list below.

(c) 'A code of business ethics in an organisation should be designed to help an individual in the organisation

- make the right choice between alternative courses of action'

- identify the appropriate person to whom an ethical dilemma should be referred'

Task 1.3

Identify whether each of the following professional accountancy bodies is or is not a sponsoring body of the AAT by selecting from the list below.

Sponsoring body of the AAT	Not a sponsoring body of the AAT

ICAI   ICAEW   ICAS   FRC   IFAC   CIMA   CIPFA   ACCA

Task 1.4

Respond to the following statement by selecting the appropriate option.

(a) The AAT Guidelines on Professional Ethics are an example of civil law.

- True
- False

Answer the following question by selecting the appropriate option.

(b) Which of the following is a valid reason for an organisation to introduce an ethical code?

- To ensure that there is consistency of conduct by employees across the organisation

- To impose criminal sanctions on employees who fail to comply with the ethical code

Task 1.5

Complete the following sentence by selecting the appropriate option from the list below.

(a) According to the Basel Committee on Banking Supervision, the definition of operational risk is:

'The risk of direct or indirect loss resulting from inadequate or failed

- processes, people and systems'
- regulation'

(b) Cecily, a member in practice, wishes to enter into a professional relationship with a client which will almost certainly last for at least two years.

Answer the following question by selecting the appropriate option.

As part of her customer due diligence processes, which of the following actions must Cecily take?

- Notify the AAT of the relationship
- Verify the nature and value of the client's assets
- Verify the client's identity on the basis of documents, data or other reliable information

Task 1.6

Complete the following sentence by selecting the most appropriate option from the list below.

(a) 'A member's continuing duty to maintain professional knowledge and skill so that a client or employer receives competent professional service forms part of the fundamental principle of

- Integrity'
- Professional competence and due care'
- Professional behaviour'

Respond to the following statement by selecting the appropriate option.

(b) Within the conceptual framework of threats and safeguards, continuing professional development (CPD) requirements form one of the safeguards created by the profession.

- True
- False

Task 1.7

(a) Jacob, an AAT member in practice, is conducting a second interview of an excellent candidate (also an AAT member) for a senior post in Jacob's firm. When discussing remuneration the potential employee states she will bring a copy of the database of clients from her old firm to introduce new clients to Jacob's firm. She also says she knows a lot of negative information about her old firm which Jacob could use to gain clients from them.

Answer the following question by selecting the appropriate option.

In order to behave in an ethical manner in these circumstances, what is the most appropriate action for Jacob to take following the interview?

- Because she shows business acumen, offer her the job

- Because she has breached the fundamental principles of integrity and confidentiality, report her to the AAT

- Because she lacks integrity, inform her that she will not be offered the job

(b) Frankie, an AAT member in practice, has been accused of bringing the profession into disrepute when marketing his professional services.

Complete the following sentence by selecting the appropriate option from the list below.

'This accusation is most likely to arise if Frankie

- states in an advertisement that he is a fully qualified member of the AAT'

- makes a disparaging reference in an advertisement to the work of Iqbal, an ACCA member'

- refers in an advertisement to the fact that some if his employees are only part-qualified'

(c) Jessica Murray is an AAT member who has worked for many years in Salim & Wright LLP, a practice that has branches in the UK, Europe and North Africa. She has now become a partner in the practice along with Tim Salim and Godfrey Wright, and Jessica wishes to change the practice's name to Salim, Wright & Murray MAAT International LLP.

Identify the element of the proposed name that is prohibited by s253 of the AAT Guidelines on Professional Ethics, by selecting it from the list below.

Permitted name				*Prohibited element*
Salim, Wright & Murray	MAAT	International	LLP	

(d)   Complete the following statement of how a member should apply safeguards against threats in any particular circumstance by selecting the appropriate word(s) from the list below.

'In exercising professional judgement, a member should consider what a reasonable and informed ————————————————————, having knowledge of all relevant information, including the ———————————————— of the threat and the safeguards applied, would conclude to be ————————————————

third party	fellow professional	cost	significance	acceptable	unacceptable

Task 1.8

(a)   Vernon, a member in practice, performs book-keeping services for both Yen Ltd and Piston Ltd. The two companies are in dispute about a series of purchases that Yen Ltd made from Piston Ltd.

Complete the following sentence by selecting the appropriate option from the list below.

'For Vernon this situation threatens both the fundamental principles of

- Objectivity and confidentiality'
- Integrity and professional behaviour'
- Confidentiality and professional competence'

(b)   Niall is a member in business. His cousin Oonagh has recently been employed by an organisation with which Niall has regular business dealings. Oonagh's position means that she would be able to offer Niall preferential treatment in the awarding of major contracts.

Answer the following question by selecting the appropriate option.

What should Niall do?

- Seek legal advice

- Advise Oonagh of relevant threats and safeguards that will protect Niall should he receive such an offer from Oonagh's organisation

- Immediately inform higher levels of management

(c)   Complete the following sentence by selecting the appropriate option from the list below.

'The requirement for an AAT member in practice to be independent of a client applies in relation to

- All clients'
- Assurance clients only'

(d)   Quentin is an AAT member in practice with Topping LLP. He is engaged on an assurance assignment for Nickel plc when he receives news that his grandmother has left him a 1% shareholding in Nickel plc in her will.

Complete the following sentence by selecting the appropriate option from the list below.

'This situation presents a

- Familiarity threat
- Self-interest threat

and the best course of action would be

- To remove Quentin from the assurance engagement'
- To inform the audit committee of Nickel plc'

(e)   Helena is employed by Elaprop LLP and has been part of an assurance team for its client, Bowen plc, for three years. Helena has been approached by Bowen plc with an offer of a senior job in the company's finance team.

Complete the following sentence by selecting the appropriate option from the list below.

'This situation presents

- an intimidation threat'
- a self-interest threat'

Answer the following question by selecting the appropriate option.

Which TWO of the following safeguards should Elaprop LLP have in place?

- A policy requiring Helena to notify the firm of such an offer

- A policy preventing Helena from entering employment negotiations with an assurance client

- A policy requiring Helena to resign from the firm once an offer of employment is received from an assurance client

- A policy requiring Helena's removal from the assurance engagement with Bowen plc

Section 2

Task 2.1

(a) Identify whether the following business values are those set out in the Nolan Principles by selecting a relevant item from the list below to each box.

Nolan Principles

Business values

Trust
Accountability
Transparency
Honesty

(b) Trevor, an AAT member, has not complied with the AAT Guidelines on Professional Ethics.

Complete the following sentence by selecting the appropriate option from the list below.

'Disciplinary action will be taken against Trevor

- Immediately'
- If his employer notifies the AAT of his non-compliance'
- If his conduct reflects adversely on the reputation of the AAT'

Task 2.2

(a) Gregory, an AAT member, has just started his own accounting business. One of his first clients, Cassandra, has asked Gregory to keep custody of £200 in cash for one month, when it will need to be paid to HM Revenue and Customs in settlement of Cassandra's income tax liability.

Answer the following question by selecting the appropriate option.

What should Gregory do?

- Keep a note of the amount of money but hold it in his established bank account

- Hold the money separately from his own money and that of his business

- Inform Cassandra that he cannot hold the money as he is not regulated by the Financial Services Authority (FSA)

(b) William is an AAT member in practice who acts on behalf of an elderly client, Jordan. Last month William issued an invoice for £5,000 to Jordan for 'safeguarding services', which just involved being sole signatory on Jordan's bank account for a period of one month. He has now transferred £7,000 to himself from Jordan's bank account, in settlement of the invoice plus £2,000 'late fees'. Following a complaint from Jordan's son, the police are now investigating William for fraud.

Answer the following question by selecting the appropriate option.

Which Fraud Act 2006 offence is it most likely that William has committed?

- Fraud by false representation
- Fraud by abuse of position
- Fraud by failing to disclose information

Task 2.3

(a) Alessandro is an AAT member in practice employed by Sueka LLP, He has acquired some information about Polina Ltd in the course of acting for the company on an assurance engagement.

Complete the following sentence by selecting the appropriate option from the list below.

'The principle of confidentiality imposes an obligation on Alessandro to refrain from

- Using the information to the advantage of Sueka LLP'
- Disclosing the information within Sueka LLP'
- Disclosing the information to anyone at all'

(b) Susan, an AAT member, owns and runs a small accountancy practice with seven employees. She has failed to notify the Information Commissioner of the practice's data processing operations.

Respond to the following statement by selecting the appropriate option.

Susan has committed a criminal offence and may be fined if convicted.

- True
- False

Task 2.4

(a) Answer the following question by selecting the appropriate option.

In which circumstance are AAT members specifically advised to seek professional advice before disclosing confidential information?

- Where there is a professional duty to disclose in the public interest, and this is not prohibited by law

- Where disclosure is required by law

- Where disclosure is permitted by law and is authorised by the client or employer

(b) Bill is an AAT member in practice as a sole practitioner. He suspects terrorist financing activities are taking place at his client, Hover Ltd.

Complete the following sentence by selecting the appropriate option from the list below.

'Bill should disclose his suspicions concerning Hover Ltd to

- The police'
- The board of Hover Ltd'
- The Serious Organised Crime Agency'

Task 2.5

(a) Complete the following sentence by selecting the appropriate option from the list below.

'Breach by a member in practice of the duty to exercise reasonable care and skill means the member may be liable to the client for

- breach of contract and professional negligence'
- fraud and professional negligence'
- fraud and breach of confidentiality'
- breach of contract and breach of confidentiality'

(b) Lionel, an AAT member in business, has been asked by his employer to undertake a major project for which Lionel currently does not have sufficient specific training or experience.

Complete the following sentence by selecting the appropriate option from the list below.

'Lionel may nonetheless undertake the project if he

- Has adequate support'
- Informs the employer that his performance will be lacking in expertise'

Task 2.6

(a) Patrick is a member in practice in the UK who acts as a principal in relation to his client, Pippa Ltd. To help Pippa Ltd's finance director in his preparation of the company's financial statements, Patrick has agreed to prepare a sales ledger control account reconciliation.

Complete the following sentence by selecting the appropriate option from the list below.

'Ownership of the reconciliation when it is complete is

- Patrick's'
- Pippa Ltd's'

(b) Identify the three conditions that must exist for an AAT member in practice to have a right of lien over the documents of a sole trader client, by selecting the relevant conditions from the list below.

Right of lien exists

Conditions

The documents belong to the client
The documents belong to a third party
The documents are in the member's possession by proper means
The documents are in the member's possession, however this has come about
Work has been done by the member on the documents for which the fee has been paid
Work has been done by the member on the documents for which the fee is outstanding

Task 2.7

(a) Zoe, an AAT member in practice in the UK, works for a large firm of accountants. Zoe has a client which refuses to make disclosure of a known error in its taxation affairs, after having had notice of the error and a reasonable time to reflect.

Complete the following sentence by selecting the appropriate option from the list below.

'Zoe is obliged to report the client's refusal and the facts surrounding it to

- HM Revenue and Customs (HMRC)'
- The Serious Organised Crime Agency (SOCA)'
- The Money Laundering Reporting Officer (MLRO)'

(b)   Respond to the following statement by selecting the appropriate option.

An act of attempting to conceal criminal property is only reportable as a money laundering offence if it involves amounts of £500 or more.

- True
- False

(c)   Complete the following sentence by inserting the appropriate figure.

'The maximum period of imprisonment that can be imposed on a person found guilty of money laundering is

—————— years'.

Task 2.8

Malcolm, an AAT member employed by Dreed plc, is facing significant pressure from his employer to intentionally mislead the company's internal auditors.

Complete the following sentence by selecting the appropriate option from each dropdown menu.

'Malcolm's situation represents

- an intimidation threat
- a self-review threat

and his immediate response should be to implement the safeguard of

- obtaining advice from the AAT'
- resigning from Dreed plc'

Task 2.9

(a)   Complete the following sentence by selecting the appropriate option from the list below.

'If an AAT member makes any disclosures which are likely to prejudice an investigation following a report to the relevant person concerning money laundering, the member

- has committed the criminal offence of tipping off'
- should consult the AAT Ethics Advice Line'
- may be liable to disciplinary action'

(b) Rohinder is an AAT member on an assurance engagement at Poster plc. During the course of the engagement he has become aware of client staff disguising the nature and source of certain funds which Rohinder believes derive from tax evasion,

Complete the following sentence by selecting the appropriate option from the list below.

'Rohinder must report his suspicions so as to avoid a charge of

- Money laundering'
- Failure to report'
- Tipping off'

Task 2.10

(a) Dominic, an AAT member, has been employed for some years by Hill plc. He feels that his immediate manager Serena poses a threat to his ability to perform his duties with the appropriate degree of professional competence and due care, as she has deliberately concealed evidence of criminal acts. Dominic has not been able to reduce this threat sufficiently with relevant safeguards. He therefore wishes to make a protected disclosure to the board of Hill plc.

Answer the following question by selecting the appropriate option.

What is Dominic's position as a whistle-blower in relation to the Public Interest Disclosure Act?

- He will not be protected unless he discloses to a legal adviser
- He will be protected provided he acts in good faith
- He will not be protected as this is not a qualifying disclosure

(b) Answer the following question by selecting the appropriate option.

To which of the following disclosures does the Public Interest Disclosure Act extend?

- Professional negligence
- Endangerment of an individual's health and safety
- Environmental damage
- Breach of contract

(c) When reporting suspicion of money laundering, an AAT member in practice must make a 'required disclosure'.

Identify which items of information should be included in the disclosure by selecting the appropriate items from the list below.

Relevant disclosure

Items of information

- The identity of the suspect (if known)
- The whereabouts of the suspect (if known)
- Information on which suspicion of money laundering is based
- The nature of the laundered property (if known)
- The whereabouts of the laundered property (if known)
- The type of money laundering offence that has been committed

SAMPLE ASSESSMENT PROFESSIONAL ETHICS IN ACCOUNTING AND FINANCE

ANSWERS

PEAF Sample Assessment

Section 1

Task 1.1

(a) Integrity'

(b) Identify, evaluate and respond to threats to compliance with the fundamental principles'

Task 1.2

(a) Acknowledgement of duties to society as a whole in addition to duties to the employer or client

(b) The Professional Oversight Board (POB)

(c) make the right choice between alternative courses of action'

Task 1.3

Sponsoring body of the AAT	Not a sponsoring body of the AAT
ICAEW	ICAI
ICAS	ACCA
CIMA	IFAC
CIPFA	FRC

Task 1.4

(a) False

(b) To ensure that there is consistency of conduct by employees across the organisation

---

Task 1.5

(a) processes, people and systems'

(b) Verify the client's identity on the basis of documents, data or other reliable information

---

Task 1.6

(a) Professional competence and due care'

(b) True

Task 1.7

(a) Because she lacks integrity, inform her that she will not be offered the job

(b) makes a disparaging reference in an advertisement to the work of Iqbal, an ACCA member'

(c)

Permitted name	Prohibited element
Salim, Wright & Murray International LLP	MAAT

(d) 'In exercising professional judgement, a member should consider what a reasonable and informed **third party**, having knowledge of all relevant information, including the **significance** of the threat and the safeguards applied, would conclude to be **unacceptable**'

Task 1.8

(a) Objectivity and confidentiality'

(b) Advise Oonagh of relevant threats and safeguards that will protect Niall should he receive such an offer from Oonagh's organisation

(c) Assurance clients only'

(d) Self-interest threat

To remove Quentin from the assurance engagement'

(e) a self-interest threat'

- A policy requiring Helena to notify the firm of such an offer

- A policy requiring Helena's removal from the assurance engagement with Bowen plc

Section 2

Task 2.1

(a) *Nolan Principles*

- Accountability
- Honesty

(b) If his conduct reflects adversely on the reputation of the AAT'

Task 2.2

(a) Hold the money separately from his own money and that of his business
(b) Fraud by abuse of position

Task 2.3

(a) Using the information to the advantage of Sueka LLP'
(b) True

Task 2.4

(a) Where there is a professional duty to disclose in the public interest, and this is not prohibited by law

(b) The Serious Organised Crime Agency

Task 2.5

(a) breach of contract and professional negligence'
(b) Has adequate support'

Task 2.6

(a) Pippa Ltd's'

(b) *Right of lien exists*

- The documents belong to the client
- The documents are in the member's possession by proper means
- Work has been done by the member on the documents for which the fee is outstanding

Task 2.7

(a)   The Money Laundering Reporting Officer (MLRO)'
(b)   False
(c)   14

Task 2.8

- an intimidation threat
- obtaining advice from the AAT'

Task 2.9

(a)   has committed the criminal offence of tipping off'
(b)   Failure to report'

Task 2.10

(a)   He will be protected provided he acts in good faith

(b)   Endangerment of an individual's health and safety

Environmental damage

(c)   Relevant disclosure

The identity of the suspect (if known)
Information on which suspicion of money laundering is based
The whereabouts of the laundered property (if known)

PRACTICE ASSESSMENT 1
PROFESSIONAL ETHICS IN ACCOUNTING AND FINANCE

Time allowed: 1 hour 30 minutes

PEAF Practice Assessment 1

Section 1

Task 1.1

(a) What is a key contributing factor to the effectiveness of an organisation's code of ethics?

- The willingness of employees to read it
- The corporate reputation of the organisation
- The level of management support 'from the top'

(b) Select the AAT's five fundamental principles of ethical behaviour from the picklist below.

Fundamental Principle

Picklist
- Confidentiality
- Accuracy
- Professional behaviour
- Courtesy
- Professional competence and due care
- Diligence
- Integrity
- Objectivity

Task 1.2

(a) What is the final stage of the AAT's Disciplinary Process?

- The Disciplinary Tribunal
- Decisions and recommendations on grounds for action
- Member's response

(b) AAT members may be liable on a number of grounds: criminal acts, breaches of trust, breach of contract, professional negligence or statutory liability (e.g. for workplace accidents).

The AAT Guidelines on Professional Ethics only deal specifically with liability arising from:

- Criminal acts
- Breach of contract
- Professional negligence

(c) Which of the following should AAT members turn to if they have an ethical dilemma and are in any doubt as to the correct course of action?

- The Financial Reporting Council
- The AAT Ethics Advice Line
- The Serious Organised Crime Agency

Task 1.3

(a) Any commission paid to an AAT member for introducing a client to another firm has to be:

- Declared to the AAT
- Kept in a client money account
- Paid to the client unless the client agrees that the AAT member can keep it

(b) Which TWO of the following circumstances prevent an AAT member from holding a client's money?

- The money is suspected criminal property
- The money exceeds £25,000
- The money is from an investment business client
- An appropriate level of interest cannot be earned from holding the money

(c) Attempting to conceal criminal property is reportable as a money laundering offence regardless of the sums involved.

- True
- False

Task 1.4

(a) Melanie, an AAT member in practice, suspects that one of her clients is engaged in deliberate tax evasion. Despite her best attempts to persuade them to undertake full and accurate disclosure of their affairs, they continue to evade their responsibilities. What can Melanie do?

- Resign from involvement in the client's tax affairs
- Report the situation to the tax authorities
- Report the situation to her firm's Money Laundering Reporting Officer

(b) Sasha, an AAT member in practice, has just taken on a new client, and is about to commence fee negotiations for a piece of financial reporting work that she has been asked to undertake. How can she make sure that she follows an ethical remuneration policy?

- Agree the basis of the fee in advance with the client

- Propose that the fee be based upon the results of the financial reporting exercise

- Tell the client that she will let them know the fee at the end of the assignment, when all of her costs are known

(c) Paige Smith is an AAT member who works for Collin & Morgan LLP, a practice that has branches in several European countries. She has now become a partner in the practice, and there are plans to change the practice's name to Collin, Morgan & Smith MAAT International LLP.

Which element of the proposed name is prohibited by s253 of the AAT Guidelines on Professional Ethics?

- International
- LLP
- MAAT

....

Task 1.5

Which of the following is an 'event' listed by the Basel Committee which represents an operational risk for business?

- Misleading reporting
- Damage to physical assets
- Professional misconduct

....

Task 1.6

(a) The taxpaying client bears ultimate responsibility for the accuracy of the data and computations in a tax return prepared by an adviser.

- True
- False

(b) Rebecca is planning to draw money out of her client's account to pay for outstanding fees. Rebecca maintains that she is owed £10,000, but the client insists that it is less. How much can Rebecca withdraw from the account?

- None – Rebecca is never allowed to touch client money, unless for a strictly specified purpose

- £10,000

- £2,000 as a reasonable part payment

- None – the client needs to agree the amount to be withdrawn

Task 1.7

(a) The partners at Brightstar LLP have worked closely with a client, Sara Ltd, for many years. They are concerned that their objectivity may be compromised after all this time, and wonder what they should do for the best.

What is the most likely threat to the fundamental ethical principle of objectivity?

- Self-review
- Familiarity
- Advocacy

... and what should be done about it?

- Rotation of personnel involved with Sara Ltd
- Establishment of mechanisms to encourage 'whistle-blowing' of staff concerns
- Quality control measures

(b) Nick, an AAT member in practice, has let slip to one of his AAT student friends that his client company is in financial difficulties. He has done this to illustrate to his friend the problems that can arise when cash controls are poor. The friend in question has some shares in the client company, and is now intending to sell them. What is the main fundamental ethical principle that Nick has violated?

- Professional competence and due care
- Confidentiality
- Professional behaviour

Task 1.8

(a)   Janice, an AAT member, is being pressured by her manager to perform a task for which she feels she does not have the appropriate level of knowledge or experience. She has told him of her concerns, but he refuses to get her any additional help or support. What should she do?

- Report her manager to the AAT as an intimidation threat

- Ask for help from a friend in another accountancy firm who has done similar work before

- Refuse to undertake the assignment

(b)   Janet, an AAT member, has been told that the future of her job depends upon the success of her company's latest product, which she knows has faults but which is being promoted widely with no mention of them. She is being asked to sell the product to her friends. What type of threat to her professional integrity does this represent?

- Self-interest
- Self-review
- Advocacy

Section 2

Task 2.1

(a) Which TWO of the following member bodies of the Consultative Committee of Accountancy Bodies are sponsoring bodies of the AAT?

- The Institute of Chartered Accountants in Ireland (ICAI)
- The Association of Chartered Certified Accountants (ACCA)
- The Chartered Institute of Management Accountants (CIMA)
- The Chartered Institute of Public Finance and Accountancy (CIPFA)

(b) A letter of engagement must specify the start and end date of an assignment.

- True
- False

Task 2.2

(a) Fiona, an AAT member offering taxation services, has told her clients that her relatively high fees are because she can promise results: her tax returns and advice have never been challenged by the taxation authorities. Is this an ethical approach?

- Yes – she has a history of good results and she can prove her expertise
- No – tax returns and advice are always open to challenge

(b) A property developer who is a client of Fay, an AAT member, has written asking whether she knows of any businesses in the city looking to sell a commercial property.

She recalls that a cinema client has told her that they are intending to sell. However, she is also aware that the value of the property will fall, once a scheme for a new entertainment complex nearby is approved. Fay knows that she cannot disclose these facts, because they are both protected by:

- Client confidentiality
- Public Interest Disclosure Act 1998
- AAT Disciplinary Regulations

Task 2.3

(a) If an AAT member prepares financial statements covering up payroll fraud, he or she is party to the concealment of 'criminal property'.

- True
- False

(b) A client has asked you to hold a significant amount of money on his behalf, pending the highly probable purchase by your client of another business.

Would you accept this money and if so how would you deal with it?

- No; the amount is likely to be too large
- No; you need to verify the purchase first
- Yes; it must be held in a separate bank account

(c) In client/adviser contracts or letters of engagement, carefully worded clauses disclaiming liability for professional negligence can be relied on as a legal protection from liability.

- True
- False

Task 2.4

(a) Which of the options below represents an example of a self-review threat?

- Financial incentives based upon results or profits
- Being asked to justify a decision that you have been involved in
- Commercial pressure

(b) Lia holds a significant number of shares in one of her firm's audit clients. The requirement to disclose these holdings, and any share trading, to the officials in charge of corporate governance in her organisation is an example of a safeguard against what kind of threat?

- Self-interest
- Self-review
- Intimidation

Task 2.5

(a) Behaving in an ethical manner involves acting with honesty, fairness and sensitivity.

Which of the following describes sensitivity?

- Treating others equally
- Respecting another's right to confidentiality and privacy
- Being truthful and avoiding the temptation to mislead or deceive others

(b) Amelia, an AAT member in practice, has been asked by a client to provide a second opinion on some work done by another firm. It appears that she will not have access to the same information that the other firm had. Give an example of a safeguard that could counteract this threat:

- Refuse to undertake the assignment
- Ask for additional help from others in her firm
- Get permission to make contact with the other firm and obtain the information

(c) When a client approaches a member in practice to perform financial reporting services, that member is bound to accept the appointment, as long as enquiries have been made of the previous adviser and there are no fees outstanding.

- True
- False

Task 2.6

Who receives the interest earned by a balance in a client money account?

- The firm holding the money
- The client
- The tax authorities

Task 2.7

(a) What can large firms do to protect conflicting client interests?

- Keep client contact details confidential
- Build 'Chinese walls' of different staff teams
- Never take on clients who are in direct competition with each other

(b) Recruitment, selection, appraisal, promotion, training and reward systems are examples of safeguards established by the professional bodies against threats to ethical principles such as objectivity.

- True
- False

Task 2.8

(a) Jemima, an AAT member, has been found guilty of fraud under the Fraud Act 2006. What punishment might she expect?

- A prison sentence only
- A prison sentence or a fine
- Payment of damages

(b) Involvement in any investment activity by AAT members in the UK requires authorisation by the

- FRC
- FSA
- AAT

(c) Fill in the missing word below.

Section 3 of the Fraud Act 2006 covers fraud by failing to .... information.

Task 2.9

(a) Which industry sector is the Basel Committee most closely associated with?

- Insurance
- Banking
- Retail

(b) Which of the following bodies can fine or impose other sanctions on accountants whose work fails to meet professional standards?

- Accounting Standards Board (ASB)
- Accountancy and Actuarial Discipline Board (AADB)
- Financial Reporting Review Panel (FRRP)

Task 2.10

(a) The threat of disciplinary action can be an effective safeguard against threats to objectivity.

- True
- False

(b) How are the AAT Guidelines on Professional Ethics related to the objectives of the accountancy profession?

- There is no particular relationship, because different bodies have drafted them

- If an accountant understands the objectives, he or she will automatically be complying with the AAT Guidelines on Professional Ethics

- The AAT Guidelines on Professional Ethics aim to assist members to achieve the objectives

PRACTICE ASSESSMENT 1
PROFESSIONAL ETHICS IN
ACCOUNTING AND FINANCE

ANSWERS

78

PEAF Practice Assessment 1

Section 1

Task 1.1

(a)   The level of management support 'from the top'

(b)

Fundamental Principle
Integrity
Objectivity
Professional competence and due care
Confidentiality
Professional behaviour

Task 1.2

(a)   The Disciplinary Tribunal

(b)   Professional negligence

(c)   The AAT Ethics Advice Line

Task 1.3

(a)   Paid to the client unless the client agrees that the AAT member can keep it.

(b)   •   It is suspected criminal property
       •   It is an investment business client

(c)   True

Task 1.4

(a)   Report the situation to her firm's Money Laundering Reporting Officer

(b)   Agree the basis of the fee in advance with the client

(c)   MAAT

Task 1.5

- Damage to physical assets

....

Task 1.6

(a) True

(b) None – the client needs to agree the amount to be withdrawn. Monies should only be drawn from the client account on the client's instruction, or for the benefit of the client

....

Task 1.7

(a) • Familiarity

  • Rotation of personnel involved with Sara Ltd

(b) Confidentiality

....

Task 1.8

(a) Refuse to undertake the assignment
(b) Self-interest

....

Section 2

Task 2.1

(a) • The Chartered Institute of Management Accountants (CIMA)
    • The Chartered Institute of Public Finance and Accountancy (CIPFA)

(b) False

Task 2.2

(a) No – tax returns and advice are always open to challenge
(b) Client confidentiality

Task 2.3

(a) True
(b) Yes; it must be held in a separate bank account
(c) False

Task 2.4

(a) Being asked to justify a decision that you have been involved in
(b) Self-interest

Task 2.5

(a) Respecting another's right to confidentiality and privacy
(b) Get permission to make contact with the other firm and obtain the information
(c) False.

Task 2.6

The client

Task 2.7

(a) Build 'Chinese walls' of different staff teams.

(b) False – they are safeguards set up *in the workplace* rather than by the professional bodies themselves.

Task 2.8

(a) A prison sentence or a fine
(b) FSA
(c) Fraud by failing to disclose information

Task 2.9

(a) Banking
(b) Accountancy and Actuarial Discipline Board (AADB)

Task 2.10

(a) True

(b) The AAT Guidelines on Professional Ethics aim to assist members to achieve the objectives

PRACTICE ASSESSMENT 2
PROFESSIONAL ETHICS IN ACCOUNTING AND FINANCE

Time allowed: 1 hour 30 minutes

Practice assessment 2: questions

PEAF Practice Assessment 2

Section 1

Task 1.1

Fill in the blank:

'The AAT Guidelines on Professional Ethics note that: 'the -------- you make in the everyday course of your professional lives can have real ethical implications.'

- Decisions
- Contacts
- Money

Task 1.2

(a) Fabio works for Clarity LLP, a firm recognised as having high ethical standards, with an ethics committee and dedicated ethics officer. He is filling out his timesheet for the week, but cannot remember how many hours he worked on an assignment for Ricotta Ltd. He decides instead to charge time to a general administrative code.

He is then questioned by one of the partners as to why his non-assigned time seems so high for the week and is told to charge more time to a large client who, the partner says, 'will never notice – remember going forward that I do not like non-chargeable time from junior staff members like you'.

How would you characterise Fabio's initial filling out of his timesheet?

- He behaved with integrity
- He was foolish to think that his time should not be charged out
- He behaved with objectivity

(b) Fabio agrees to amend his timesheet. What type of threat to fundamental ethical principles did the partner's words represent?

- Self interest
- Familiarity
- Intimidation

(c) If Fabio is uncomfortable with this turn of events, what is he advised to do?

- Seek advice from his firm's ethics committee
- Complain about the partner to his department manager
- Resign from his position

Task 1.3

(a) Gavin, an AAT member, has just established his own practice and wants to offer referral fees to third parties to help him to get some new clients. He is proposing a fee of £1,000 per client that is successfully referred.

What is Gavin's position with this policy?

- It is acceptable as long as the referred client is aware of the fee and agrees to it being paid

- It is unacceptable because it represents a threat to the objectivity of the third parties involved

- £1,000 is too high a fee

(b) Which of the following best illustrates the principle behind managing conflicts of interest?

- You can never take on clients with conflicting interests

- The interests of one client must not have a negative effect on the interests of another

- It is impossible to fully manage the interests of more than one client at a time

Task 1.4

Fill in the blanks using the words in the table below

'A letter of engagement provides written -------- of the agreement with the client as to the nature and -------- of the work to be undertaken, and the -------- of both the client and the accountant in the relationship'

evidence	duties	scope	confirmation	cost	responsibilities

Task 1.5

(a) As an AAT member in practice, what should you do if a statutory demand for information on one of your clients is made?

- Hand over all of the required information straight away
- Seek legal advice
- Recommend that your client complies with the information request

(b) Henry's client, George Ltd, is putting directors' private expenditure through its tax return as a business expense, in an attempt to reduce its tax liability.

What should Henry do?

- Adjust the tax return to remove the private expenditure
- Explain his professional obligations – he cannot endorse a misleading tax return
- Ignore the private expenditure – his job is to get the best result he can for George Ltd

Task 1.6

(a) What are the main general principles governing how AAT members advertise their professional services?

- Effectiveness and integrity
- Integrity and professional behaviour
- Integrity and dignity

(b) 'Holders of public office have a duty to declare any private interests relating to their public duties and to take steps to resolve any conflicts arising in a way that protects the public interest.' Which of the Nolan Principles is being defined here?

- Selflessness
- Openness
- Honesty

(c) You have received a letter from a landlord, requesting financial information about one of your individual clients, who is applying to rent a property. The information is needed as soon as possible, by fax or e-mail, in order to secure approval for the client.

What ethical principle does this situation raise?

- Professional competence and due care
- Confidentiality
- Professional behaviour

Task 1.7

(a) Ideally, how should minor ethical issues at work be resolved?

- Consultation with the AAT Ethics Advice Line
- Informal discussion with your immediate manager
- Consultation with the Accountancy and Actuarial Discipline Board

(b) What form of monitoring is the one largely adopted by the accountancy profession in the UK?

- Self-regulation
- Independent watchdog
- Government regulation

(c) Failure to comply with a professional code of practice can result in:

- Breach of contract and damages
- Professional negligence
- Expulsion from the relevant professional organisation

(d) If safeguards in the workplace are insufficient to counter a threat to one of the fundamental ethical principles, what should an AAT member do?

- Seek legal advice
- Refuse to act
- Report concerns to the AAT Director of Professional Development

Task 1.8

(a) Rowan, an AAT member in practice, has been offered a job by his client, Greene Ltd. What should he do as a first step, before considering the offer?

- Inform his manager that such an offer has been made
- Immediately resign from his current position
- Refuse the offer, as he is not allowed to accept it

(b) Billy, an AAT member in practice, has just moved to expensive new offices in the centre of a major city. He enjoys the prestige associated with them, but is worried about the rental cost and proposes that he increase his charge-out rates to cover it.

Is this ethical?

- Yes, it is acceptable to cover office overheads in charge-out rates
- No, he chose to move to new offices and clients should not have to pay for them

Section 2

Task 2.1

(a) There is suspicion on the part of an AAT member that her client has supplied information for a tax return, recently prepared and submitted by the member, without checking the details.

Does the adviser have an ethical issue?

- No – it is the client's responsibility as they have not checked the information

- Yes – the adviser is in the position of supplying inaccurate or misleading information to HMRC

(b) Disclosure of suspected money laundering is:

- A legal duty
- A professional duty
- Acceptable as long as confidentiality is respected

Task 2.2

(a) Tom, an AAT member in practice, has just discovered that his friend has been offered a lucrative supply contract by a large company, which is a client of Tom's firm. Having prepared its accounts, Tom is aware that the company is in serious financial difficulties – to the point that it may not be able to meet its financial obligations.

Can Tom disclose anything to his friend?

- Yes, as he has prepared the accounts and they will soon be public knowledge anyway

- No, he cannot breach the confidentiality of his client

(b) What action could Tom take?

- Encourage his friend to accept a contract from another company that he knows is in better financial shape

- Encourage his friend to exercise due diligence before accepting any contract

- Report the client to the Financial Reporting Council for entering into contracts that it may not be able to honour

(c) What fundamental ethical principle must be balanced against the benefits of disclosure of matters in the public interest?

- Objectivity
- Integrity
- Confidentiality

Task 2.3

(a) Ajay, an AAT member in practice, has been asked to prepare a bank reconciliation for a charity client of his firm. Ajay has never prepared a bank reconciliation for a charity before, but the accountant at the charity knows Ajay from her previous job and is happy to work with him. What threat to his professional competence does this piece of work represent?

- No threat – a bank reconciliation is not likely to be sector specific and Ajay should be equal to the task

- A threat – Ajay has never worked for a charity in this capacity before

- A threat – Ajay knows the accountant and this will affect his ability to perform the reconciliation properly

(b) Charlie's main selling point for his new practice is his low fee rate. He currently has more clients than other practices of a similar size, and plans to recruit more staff. Last week he discovered an error in a tax return that he prepared recently.

What does this scenario illustrate?

- If low fees are charged, you need to make sure that you can still offer a quality service

- Low fees always mean a low quality service

- Low fees always work well in attracting customers

What should Charlie do about the error in tax return?

- Leave it until next year when he will have more staff
- Charge the client an extra fee to correct the error that he made
- Advise the client that the relevant tax authority must be notified of the error

Task 2.4

Fill in the blanks in the following AAT definition of misconduct, using words from the table.

'[having] conducted him/herself in such a manner as would in the opinion of the ------ or the Disciplinary Tribunal prejudice his/her status as a ------ or reflect adversely on the ------- of the Association.'

Investigations Team	member	ethics	Serious Organised Crime Agency	reputation	professional

Task 2.5

(a) Stuart has been working for Pynn LLP for a year, since leaving Angus Ltd where he was an accountant in the marketing department. Angus Ltd has just appointed Pynn LLP to be its advisers and has asked the firm to undertake a financial reporting assignment. Should Stuart be involved on the assignment?

- No – there is a self-review threat here
- Yes – as long as he abides by the fundamental ethical principles
- No – he cannot be trusted to be objective

(b) Significant levels of unpaid fees from a client can constitute a threat to your objectivity and independence.

- True
- False

Task 2.6

(a) Fill in the blank:

Under UK law the ownership of working papers in respect to taxation services normally resides with:

- The accountant
- The client
- HMCE

(b) 'All professional and business judgements should be made fairly.'

This statement is a definition of which ethical principle?

- Integrity
- Objectivity
- Professional behaviour

Task 2.7

(a) Fill in the missing word below.

Section 2 of the Fraud Act 2006 covers fraud by .... representation.

(b) When advertising his or her practice, an AAT member must never make comparisons with competitors.

- True
- False

Task 2.8

(a) Fill in the blank:

'-------- risk is that arising from the carrying out of a company's business'

- Reputational
- Strategic
- Operational

(b) Fill in the blank:

Due care is a legal concept which states that, having accepted an assignment, you have ------- to carry it out to the best of your ability.

- A contractual obligation
- An ethical duty
- A set amount of time

Task 2.9

Jenny, an AAT member in practice, has attended a seminar on ethics in the workplace. One of her colleagues made the statement: 'Ethics are black and white, and everyone needs to come to an agreement when an ethical issue arises at work.'

Is this statement correct?

- Yes
- No

Task 2.10

Which TWO of the following does the accountancy profession list as objectives?

- The mastering of particular skills and techniques
- Achieving the best possible outcomes for clients
- Development of an ethical approach to work
- Acknowledgement of duties to the financial services industry

PRACTICE ASSESSMENT 2
PROFESSIONAL ETHICS IN ACCOUNTING AND FINANCE

ANSWERS

PEAF Practice Assessment 2

Section 1

Task 1.1

Decisions

....

Task 1.2

(a) He behaved with integrity
(b) Intimidation
(c) Seek advice from his firm's ethics committee

....

Task 1.3

(a) It is acceptable as long as the referred client is aware that the fee and agrees to it being paid
(b) The interests of one client must not have a negative effect on the interests of another.

....

Task 1.4

A letter of engagement provides written **evidence** of the agreement with the client as to the nature and **scope** of the work to be undertaken, and the **responsibilities** of both the client and the accountant in the relationship.

....

Task 1.5

(a) Seek legal advice
(b) Explain his professional obligations – he cannot endorse a misleading tax return

....

Task 1.6

(a) Integrity and dignity
(b) Honesty
(c) Confidentiality

....

Task 1.7

(a)   Informal discussion with your immediate manager
(b)   Self-regulation
(c)   Expulsion from the relevant professional organisation
(d)   Refuse to act

Task 1.8

(a)   Inform his manager that such an offer has been made
(b)   Yes, it is acceptable to cover office overheads in charge-out rates

Section 2

Task 2.1

(a) Yes – the adviser is in the position of supplying inaccurate or misleading information to HMRC

(b) A legal duty

Task 2.2

(a) No, he cannot breach the confidentiality of his client
(b) Encourage his friend to exercise due diligence before accepting any contract
(c) Confidentiality

Task 2.3

(a) No threat – a bank reconciliation is not likely to be sector specific and Ajay should be equal to the task

(b) • If low fees are charged, you need to make sure that you can still offer a quality service

• Advise the client that the relevant tax authority must be notified of the error

Task 2.4

'[having] conducted him/herself in such a manner as would in the opinion of the **Investigations Team** or the Disciplinary Tribunal prejudice his/her status as a **member** or reflect adversely on the **reputation** of the Association'.

Task 2.5

(a) No – there is a self-review threat here
(b) True

Task 2.6

(a)   The accountant
(b)   Objectivity

Task 2.7

(a)   Fraud by false representation
(b)   False

Task 2.8

(a)   Operational
(b)   A contractual obligation

Task 2.9

No.

Task 2.10

* The mastering of particular skills and techniques
* Development of an ethical approach to work

Notes

Notes

Notes

Notes